DELTA YOUNG LEARNERS ENGLISH

Super Starters

An activity-based course for young learners

Pupil's Book

Wendy Superfine and Judy West

Super Starters

DELTA Publishing
Quince Cottage
Hoe Lane
Peaslake
Surrey GU5 9SW
United Kingdom

Email: superstarters@deltapublishing.co.uk
www.deltapublishing.co.uk

© Delta Publishing 2006

All rights reserved. No reproduction, copy or transmission of this publication may be made without written permission from the publishers or in accordance with the provisions of the Copyright, Designs and Patents Act 1988.

First published 2006
Reprinted 2010, 2011

Project managed by Chris Hartley
Edited by Karen Gray
Designed by Peter Bushell
Illustrations by Claire Mumford and Andy Hammond
Photographs by Michael Little Photography, with thanks to Reigate Priory School
Printed in China by RR Donnelley

ISBN-10: 1 905085 01 X
ISBN-13: 978 1 905085 01 9

Contents

Alphabet Fun the alphabet — 4

UNIT 1 Hello Kim and Sam! colours, numbers, greetings — 6

UNIT 2 Clothes clothes, *What's this/that?*, *There's/There are* — 14

UNIT 3 Face and body body parts, *have got*, present continuous — 22

UNIT 4 The family family members, *Who's this? It's …* — 30

UNIT 5 Transport transport, prepositions, *have got* — 38

UNIT 6 Animals animals, *I'm …*, *can/can't*, action verbs — 46

UNIT 7 The classroom school objects, prepositions, *Where's the …?* — 54

UNIT 8 Sport and hobbies sports/hobbies, present continuous, *like/don't like*, verbs — 62

UNIT 9 Food and drink foods and drinks, *like/don't like*, present simple — 70

UNIT 10 In the house rooms and furniture, adjectives, *There's/There are* — 78

The Super Starters Snake game revision boardgame — 86

Alphabet fun

4

UNIT 1 Hello, Kim and Sam!

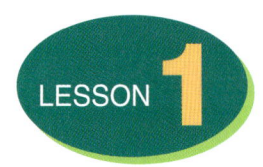

LESSON 1

1 Listen and repeat

2 Read and say *yes* or *no*

1 Kim and Sam are friends.
2 There are numbers on the wheel.
3 There are animals on the wheel.
4 Sam can count to ten.
5 Kim can count to ten.

3 Say, count and spell

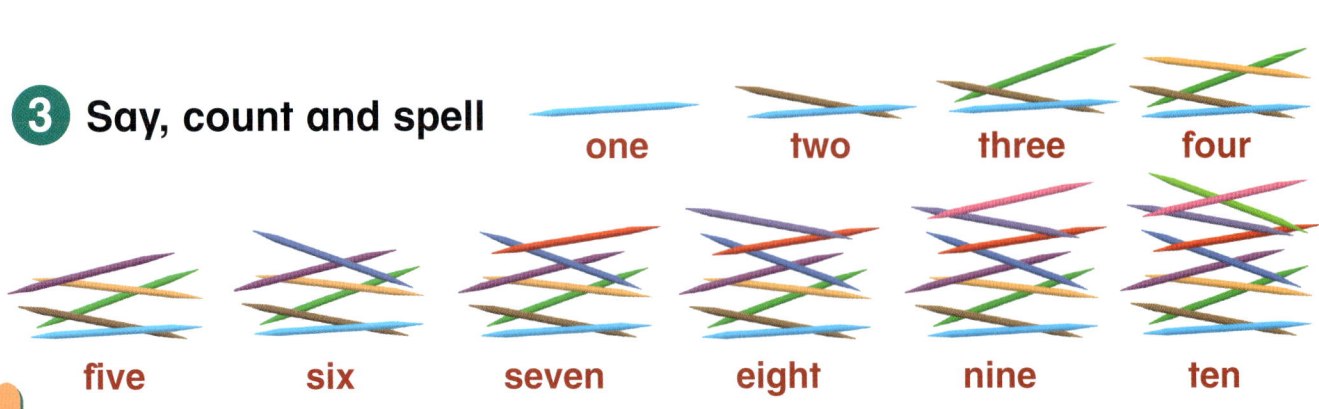

one   two   three   four

five   six   seven   eight   nine   ten

UNIT 1

LESSON 3

Can you make this?

1 Make a colour wheel → Activity Book cut-out 1

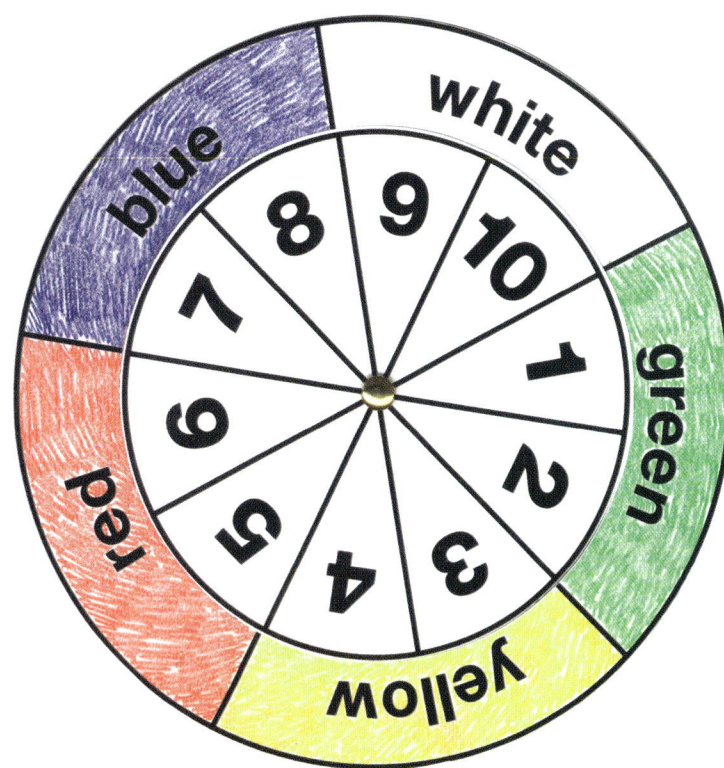
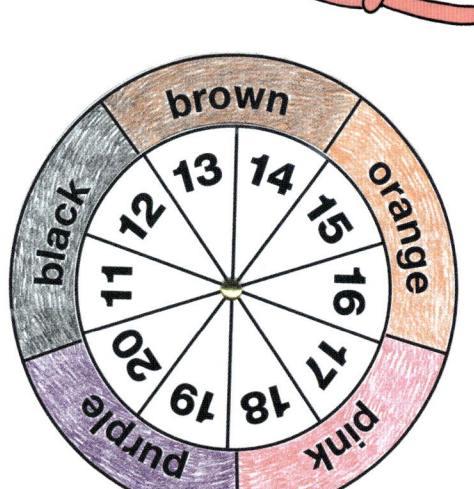

2 Listen and say 🎧 4

Green : one and two.
Yellow : three and four.
Red : five and six.
Blue : seven and eight.
White : nine and ten.

3 Do it together

What colour's nine?   It's white.   What colour's two?   It's green.

1 **Listen, look and say** *yes* **or** *no* 🎧 5

2 **Write together**

3 **Play a game**

UNIT 1　　LESSON 5

1 Listen and look 🎧 6

What colour's the big book?

It's green.

2 Listen, choose and answer together 🎧 7

brown　　black　　pink

orange　　grey

3 Read and point

Point to the desk.
Point to the board.
Point to the window.
Point to the door.

Point to the desk.

LESSON 6

1 Look again

Number four isn't on the board.

2 Match the questions and answers

1 What's on the chair?
2 What colour is the eraser?
3 Is the doll on the chair?
4 How many books are on the table?
5 Is the big book green?

a No, it's on the floor.
b No, it's pink.
c Three books.
d It's a ball.
e It's grey.

3 Let's play a counting game

One red.

One red, two blue.

One red, two blue, three orange.

11

UNIT 1 — LESSON 7

1 Point and say

A is red.

V is grey.

G and Q are yellow.

K, P and X are pink.

2 Ask and answer

1 Is Q yellow or blue?
2 Is W green or brown?
3 Is T red or blue?
4 Are K and X green or pink?
5 Are H and N yellow or black?
6 Are U and R purple or grey?

3 Say *yes* or *no*

1 Bananas are yellow.
2 Milk is green.
3 Grapes are blue.
4 Lemons are yellow.

1 Listen and say 🎧 8

| see me | blue you |

2 Listen and sing 🎧 9

1. Look, look, can you see?
   There's a little bird,
   Looking at me.
   There's one egg,
   One *blue* egg.

2. Look, look, can you see?
   There's a little bird,
   Looking at me.
   There's one egg,
   One *yellow* egg.

3. Look, look, can you see?
   There's a little bird,
   Looking at me.
   There's one egg,
   One *green* egg.

4. Look, look, can you see?
   There's a little bird,
   Looking at me.
   There's one egg,
   One *red* egg.

   One, two, three, four eggs!
   Blue, yellow, green, red eggs!

3 Play a game

I'm blue.   I'm green.   I'm red.   I'm purple.

UNIT 2 Clothes

LESSON 1

1 Listen and repeat 🎧 10

2 Read and say *yes* or *no*

1 Kim has got a hat.
2 Sam's making a hat.
3 The hat's big.
4 The hat's for Kim's doll.
5 Dogs wear hats.

3 Say and spell

doll not **dog**   **hat** not **cat**   **shirt** not **skirt**

1. Listen and point 🎧 11

2. Say together

There's a shirt.   There are shoes.
There's a dress. There are trousers.
There's a skirt. There are two hats.

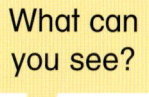

What can you see?

3. Listen, point and spell 🎧 12

1 **Make a cut-out doll** ➡ Activity Book cut-out 2   ➡ Teacher's Book page P4

2 **Listen and say** 🎧 13

He's wearing a blue T-shirt.
She's wearing a purple skirt.
He's wearing brown trousers.
She's wearing a pink T-shirt.

3 **Do it together**

1 Listen, look and say *yes* or *no* 🎧 14

2 Write together

3 Play a game

1 Listen and look 🎧 15

2 Listen, choose and answer together 🎧 16

handbag   jacket   shoes   glasses

Point to the shoes under the bed.

3 Read and point

Point to the shoes under the bed.
Point to the hat on the chair.
Point to the dress on the bed.
Point to the socks in the cupboard.

LESSON 6

UNIT 2

1 Look again

The handbag's on the table.

2 Match the questions and answers

1 Where's the mouse?   a It's on the chair.
2 What colour are the socks?   b It's in the cupboard.
3 Where's the jacket?   c Two.
4 What colour is the hat?   d They're blue.
5 How many shoes are under the chair?   e It's red.

3 Let's play *Pass the hat*

That's my hat!

Sit down, stand up and pass the hat!

LESSON 7

1 Point and say

Look. The jackets are next to the jeans.

2 Ask and answer

1 What colour's Kim's T-shirt?
2 Is she wearing a blue skirt?
3 Is she wearing glasses?
4 Is Sam wearing a jacket?
5 What colour are Sam's shoes?
6 What's he looking at?

3 Answer for you

1 Are you wearing a blue hat?
2 Are you wearing jeans?
3 Is your friend wearing jeans?
4 Are you wearing a shirt?
5 Is your teacher wearing a jacket?

LESSON 8

1 Listen and say 🎧 17

| dress   yes | hat   cat | blue   you |

2 Listen and sing 🎧 18 ♪♫♪♫

Here's my hat,

Yellow and blue.

Here's my shirt,

Here's my shoe.

Here's my T-shirt.

Here's my dress.

Can you see it? No or yes?

Can you see my trousers, too?

All my clothes are yellow or blue!

3 Play *Guess the clothes*

Is it a hat?

Is it blue?

UNIT 3 Face and body

1 Listen and repeat  19

2 Read and say *yes* or *no*

1 Kim is painting her monster.
2 Fred is a monster.
3 His face is orange.
4 His ears are orange.
5 His nose is black.

3 Say and spell

| eye | face | nose | mouth |

LESSON 2

UNIT 3

1. Listen and point 🎧 20

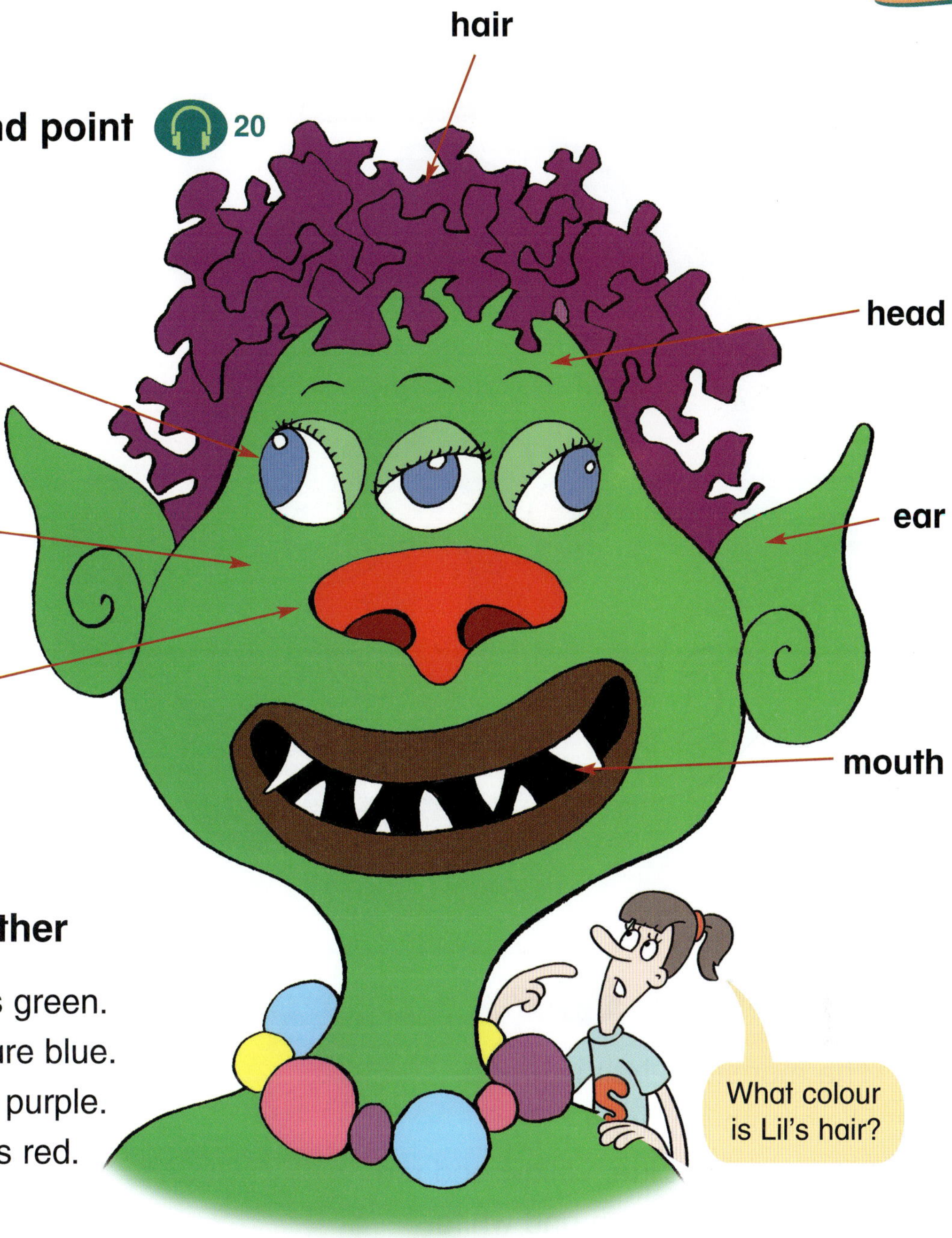

hair

eye

head

face

ear

nose

mouth

2. Say together

Lil's face is green.
Lil's eyes are blue.
Lil's hair is purple.
Lil's nose is red.

What colour is Lil's hair?

3. Listen, point and spell 🎧 21

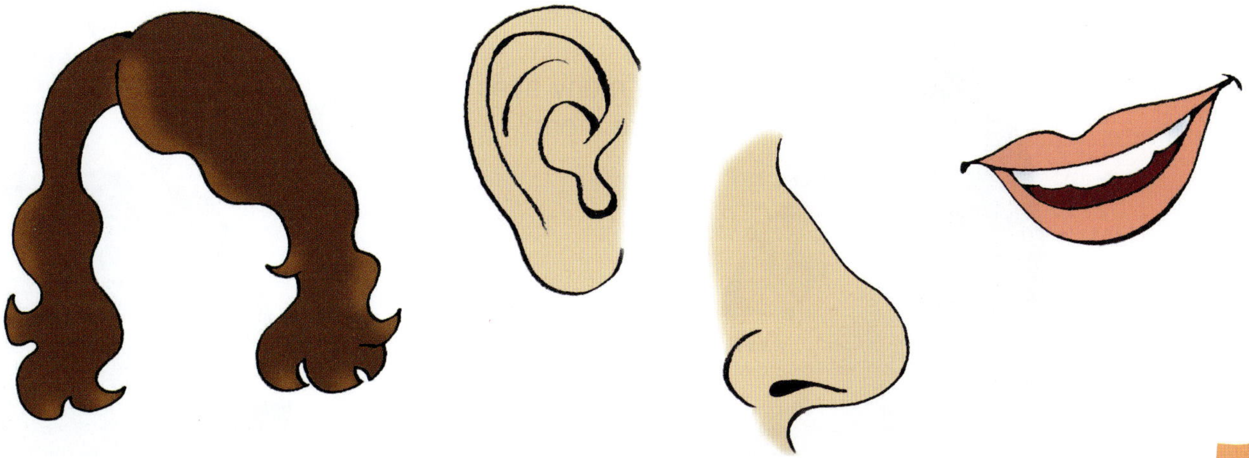

1 Make a monster mask → Activity Book cut-out 3   → Teacher's Book page P6

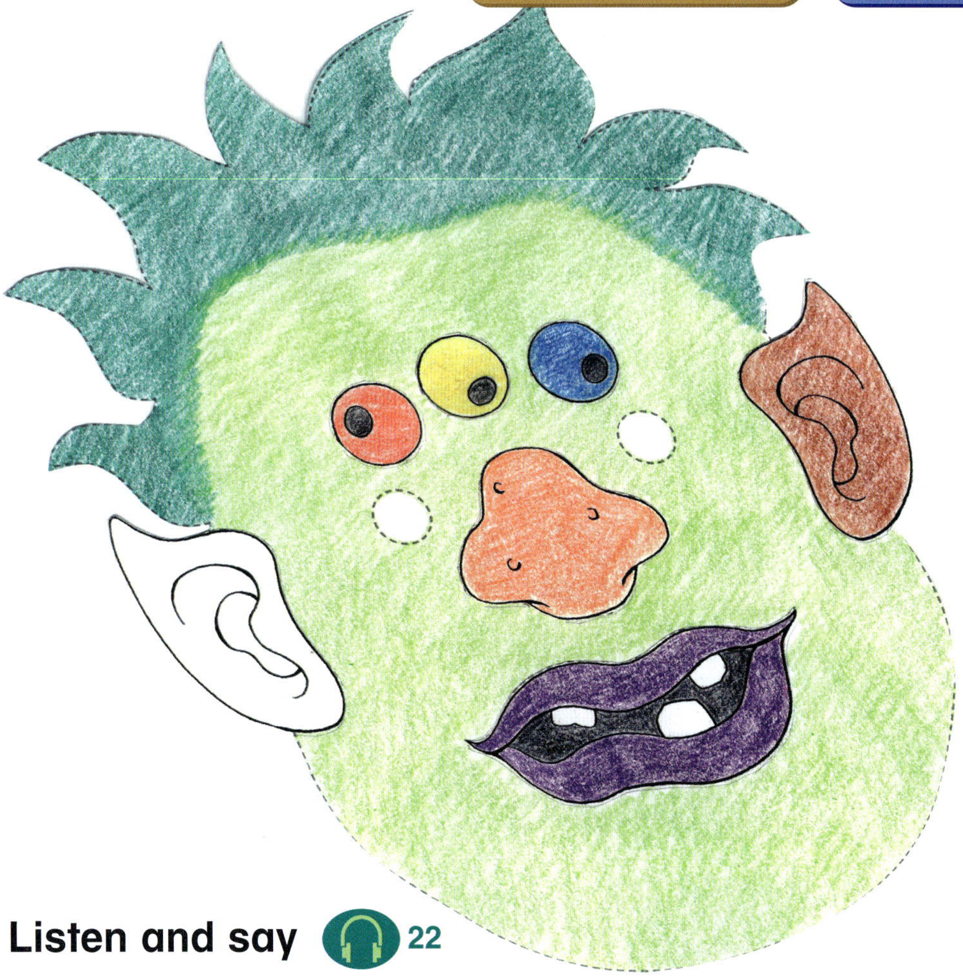

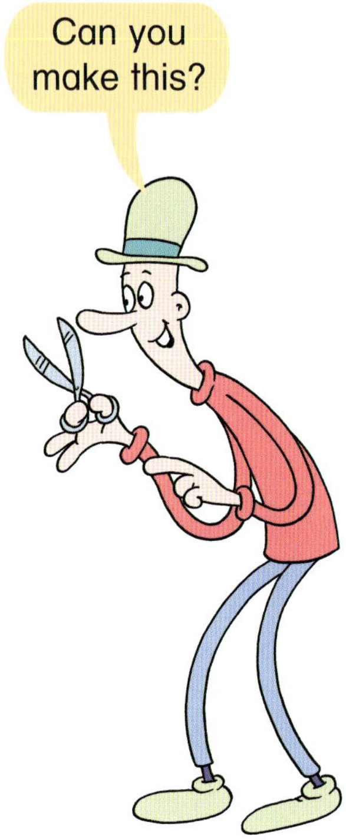

2 Listen and say 🎧 22

1 The monster's hair is green.
2 His mouth is purple.
3 His eyes are blue, yellow and red.
4 His ears are brown and white.

3 Do it together

What colour's your monster's hair? — Blue.
How many eyes are there? — Two.
What's your monster's name? Spell it. — Anto. A-n-t-o.

UNIT 3

LESSON 5

"The green monster's flying a kite."

1 Listen and look 🎧 24

2 Listen, choose and answer together 🎧 25

"Look at the yellow monster."

- green monster
- pink monster
- blue monster
- yellow monster
- red monster

3 Read and point

Point to the pink monster.
Point to the monster with short arms.
Point to the monster with long legs.
Point to the kite.
Point to the dog.

LESSON 6

UNIT 3

"The pink monster's very big."

1 Look again

2 Match the questions and answers

1 What's the dog doing?
2 What's the red monster doing?
3 How many monsters are there?
4 Where's the ball?
5 Are the green monster's legs big?

a He's sleeping.
b There are four.
c No, they aren't.
d It's running.
e It's in the dog's mouth.

3 Let's play *The monster's got …*

"The monster's got two eyes."

"The monster's got two eyes and ten legs."

UNIT 3 — LESSON 7

1 Point and say

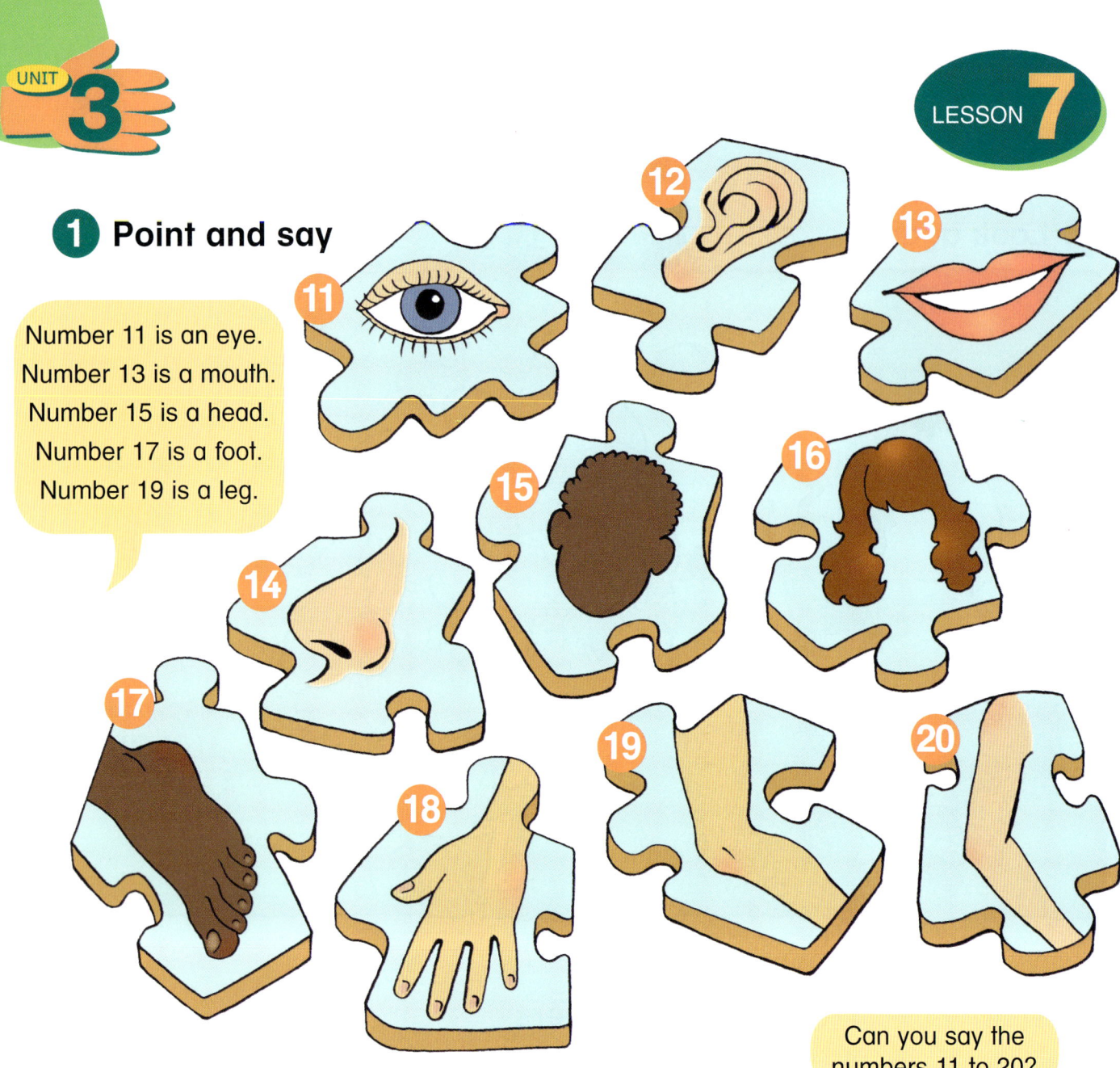

Number 11 is an eye.
Number 13 is a mouth.
Number 15 is a head.
Number 17 is a foot.
Number 19 is a leg.

Can you say the numbers 11 to 20?

2 Ask and answer

1. Is number 12 an ear?
2. Is number 14 a mouth?
3. Is number 16 hair or a head?
4. Is number 18 a foot or a hand?
5. Is number 20 a leg or an arm?

3 Say *yes* or *no*

1. Have you got blue eyes?
2. Have you got black hair?
3. Have you got two feet?
4. Have you got six legs?
5. Have you got big feet?
6. Has your friend got brown eyes?

LESSON 8

UNIT 3

1 Listen and say 🎧 26

| twenty   two | thirteen   three | fifteen   five |

2 Listen and sing 🎧 27

Here's my monster.
His name is Moo.
He's very ugly,
And purple, too.

Here's my monster.
His eyes are blue.
His ears are yellow.
His nose is, too.

Funny feet and a funny face.
Funny monster, Monster Moo!

3 Play *Draw the monster!*

"Draw two eyes, please."

UNIT 4 The family

1 Listen and repeat

2 Read and say *yes* or *no*

1. Sam's making a family photo card.
2. Kim's putting photos in the card.
3. Kim's grandfather is Ted.
4. Sam's making a card for his grandmother.
5. Kim lives in her grandfather's house.

3 Say and spell

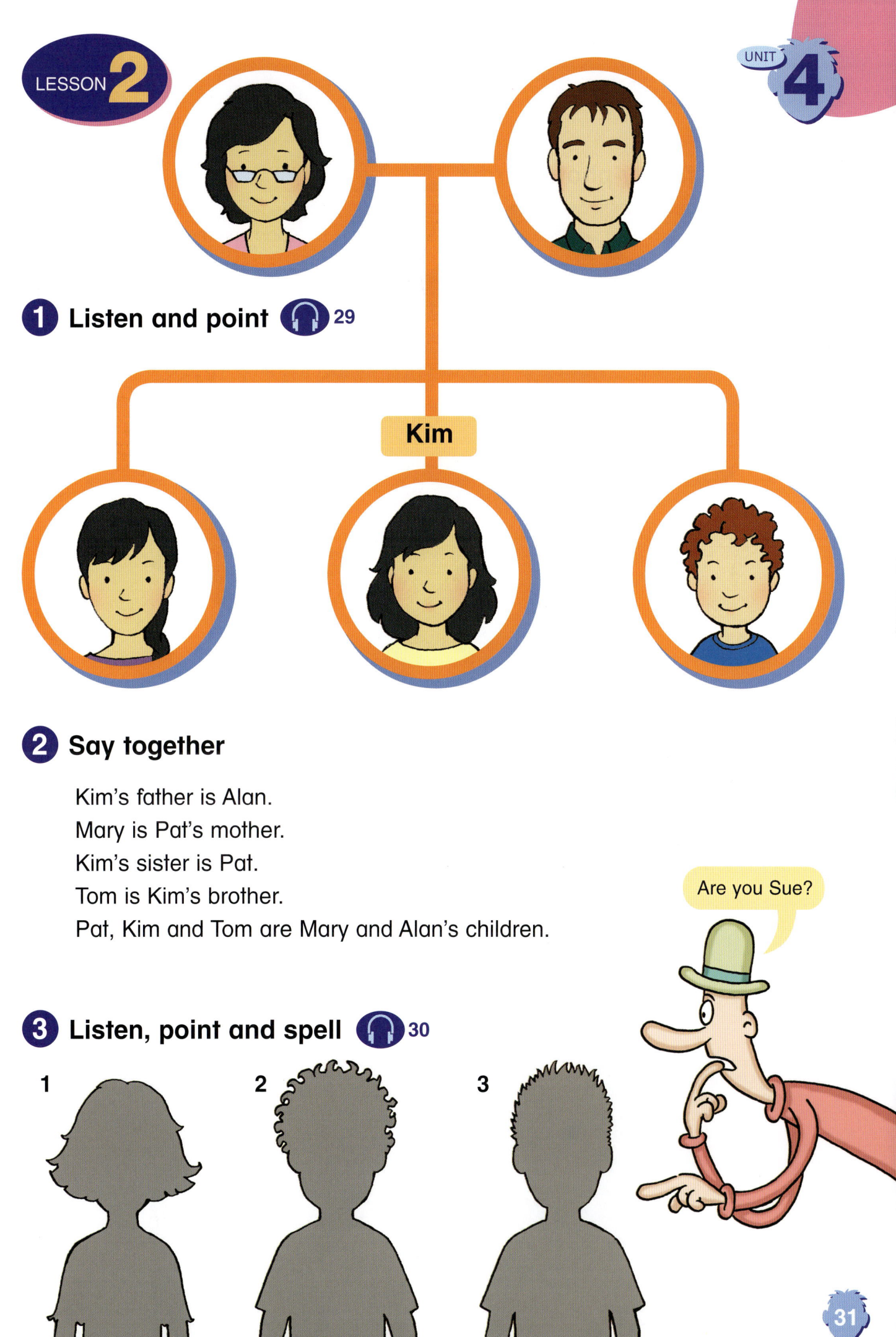

LESSON 2

1 Listen and point 🎧 29

2 Say together

Kim's father is Alan.
Mary is Pat's mother.
Kim's sister is Pat.
Tom is Kim's brother.
Pat, Kim and Tom are Mary and Alan's children.

Are you Sue?

3 Listen, point and spell 🎧 30

1 2 3

1 Make a family photo card

Can you make this?

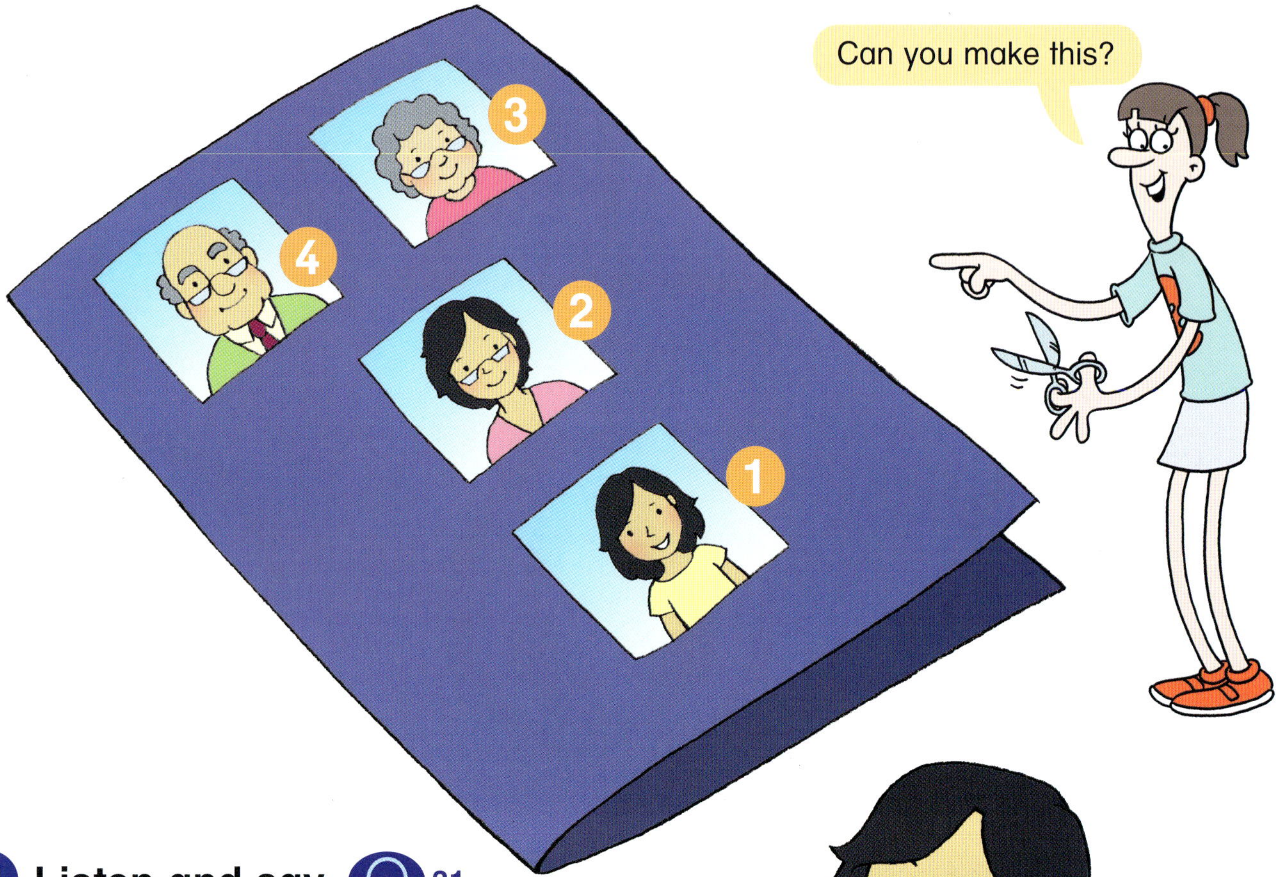

2 Listen and say 🎧 31

Photo number 1 is me!
Photo number 2 is my mother.
My grandmother is number 3.
My grandfather is number 4.

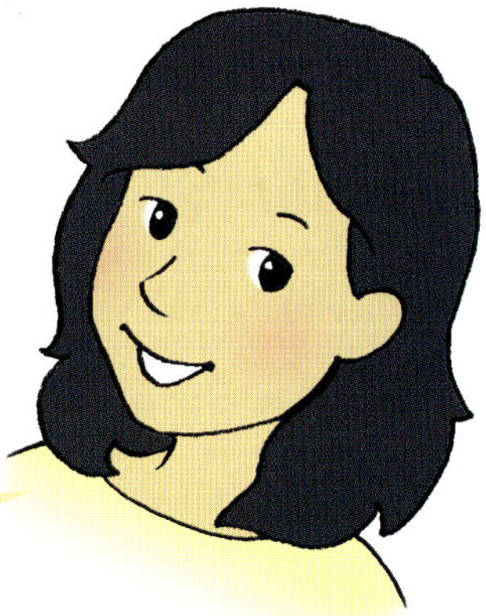

3 Do it together

Who's this?

It's my father.

LESSON 4

1 Listen, look and say *yes* or *no* 🎧 32

"What are they doing?"

2 Write together

"Sister." "s-i-s-t-e-r" *sister*

3 Play a game

"Mime together." "What are we doing?"

UNIT 4

LESSON 5

1 Listen and look 🎧 33

Who's that?

That's my mum's sister.

2 Listen, choose and answer together 🎧 34

Kim   Ben   Kim's mother   Kim's grandmother

3 Read and point

Point to the cake.
Point to the bookcase.
Point to the clock.
Point to Kim's grandmother.

Is she young or old?

LESSON 6

1 Look again

2 Match the questions and answers

1 What's Ben doing now?
2 What's Kim's grandmother doing?
3 What are Tony and Sid doing?
4 Where's Kim's father?
5 What's he doing?

a They're eating ice cream.
b He's watching TV.
c He's sleeping under the table.
d He's sitting in the armchair.
e She's looking at the photo card.

3 Let's play *What have I got?*

LESSON 7

1 Point and say

My mum's name is Mary. Her sister is Lucy. I like Lucy. Lucy's got one child. He's a boy. His name's Ben. Ben's my cousin. He's only three. He likes cats.

2 Ask and answer

1 Who's Kim's mum?
2 What's her sister's name?
3 How many children has Lucy got?
4 What's his name?
5 How old is he?
6 How old is Kim?

How old are you?

3 Answer for you

1 Have you got a sister?
2 Have you got a brother?
3 Have you got six cousins?
4 Are you eight years old?
5 Is your brother nine years old?
6 What's your dad's name?

LESSON 8 — UNIT 4

1 Listen and say 🎧 35

- man   men
- woman   women
- child   children
- person   people

2 Listen and sing 🎧 36

Happy Birthday, Grandma

1. Come now, come here please,
   Come for the family photo.
   Mummy, Daddy, smile please.
   Smile for the photo.

2. Come now, come here please,
   Come for the family photo.
   Grandpa, Grandma, smile please.
   Smile for the photo.

3. Come now, come here please,
   Come for the family photo.
   Sister, brother, smile please.
   Smile for the photo.

4. Come here everyone,
   Come for the family photo.
   Come here, smile please.
   Smile for the photo.

Say 'cheese' please!

3 Play *Don't smile!*

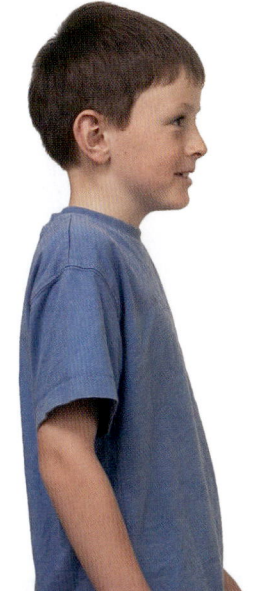

Are you a boy?
Are you eight years old?
Are you in Class 4?
Is your face green?

UNIT 5 Transport

1 Listen and repeat 🎧 37

2 Read and say *yes* or *no*

1. It's Sam's bike.
2. Kim likes the red bike.
3. Kim's favourite colour is red.
4. Tony's driving a car.
5. Tony's riding a motorbike.

3 Say and spell

bus   plane   car   bike

1 Listen and point  38

2 Say together

The motorbike's behind the red car.
The black bike's in front of the red car.
The plane's above the motorbike.
The bus is behind the yellow bike.
The green car's between the black bike and the bus.

3 Listen, point and spell  39

1

2

3

4

Do you know these words?

UNIT 5 — LESSON 3

1 Make a street picture ➡ Activity Book cut-out 5

Can you make this?

2 Listen and say 🎧 40

I'm making a street picture.
I've got a bus but I haven't got a motorbike.
I've got a car but I haven't got a boat.

3 Do it together

What colour's your car?

Green. Where's your lorry?

It's behind the motorbike.

1 Listen, look and say *yes* or *no*

2 Write together

3 Play a game

UNIT 5

LESSON 5

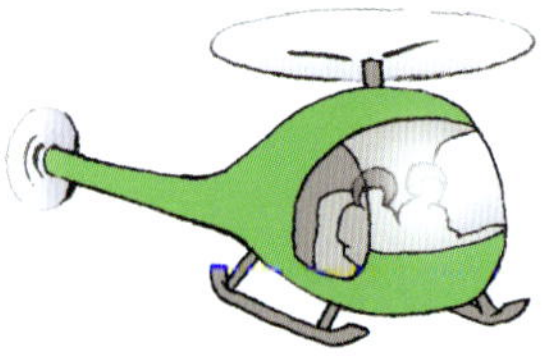

1 Listen and look 🎧 42

Can you see a bus?
What colour is it?

It's red.

2 Listen, choose and answer together 🎧 43

Tony   red   a helicopter
waving   behind the car

3 Read and point

Point to the man on the black motorbike.
Point to the red bus.
Point to the children with the dog.
Point to the boy eating an ice cream.
Point to the helicopter.

Point to the boat.

42

 LESSON 6

 UNIT 5

1 Look again

There isn't a bus. There's a lorry.

2 Match the questions and answers

1 Is Tony riding his bike?
2 Is the man driving the blue car?
3 Where's the red lorry?
4 What colour are the motorbikes?
5 Is the lorry window open or closed?

a It's in front of the blue car.
b It's open.
c No, he's riding his motorbike.
d No, he isn't.
e They're green and red.

3 Let's play *Where's the helicopter?*

Put the helicopter on the chair.

1 Point and say

Tony Mr White Mrs White Ben

1   2   3   4

a
b
c
d

2 Ask and answer

1 Whose bike is very new?
2 Whose bike is very small?
3 Whose bike is black and grey?
4 Whose bike is very old?
5 Whose bike is red?

This is Kim's bike.

3 Say *yes* or *no*

1 Have you got a bike?
2 Is your bike red?
3 Has your mother got a bike?
4 Is her bike new?
5 Has your grandfather got a bike?
6 Is his bike very old?

1 Listen and say 🎧 44

| fly   my | plane   train | bus   us |

2 Listen and sing 🎧 45 ♪♪♪♪

I fly in a plane.
I sit in a train.
But most of all I like my bike,
I ride my bike … all day long.

I go in a boat.
I drive in a car.
But most of all I like my bike,
I ride my bike … all day long.

I go by helicopter,
Or by bus.
But most of all I like my bike,
I ride my bike … all day long.

3 Play *Word train*

UNIT 6 # Animals

LESSON 1

1 Listen and repeat  46

2 Read and say *yes* or *no*

1 The bird can fly.
2 The bird can walk.
3 The bird can swim.
4 It's a chicken.
5 They've got four eggs.

3 Say and spell

fish   chicken   dog   goat

LESSON 2

UNIT 6

1 Listen and point 🎧 47

2 Say together

A mouse can run.
A sheep can't sing.
A cow can eat.
A duck can swim and it can fly.
A horse can jump but it can't sing.

3 Listen, point and spell 🎧 48

Can you spell *sheep*?

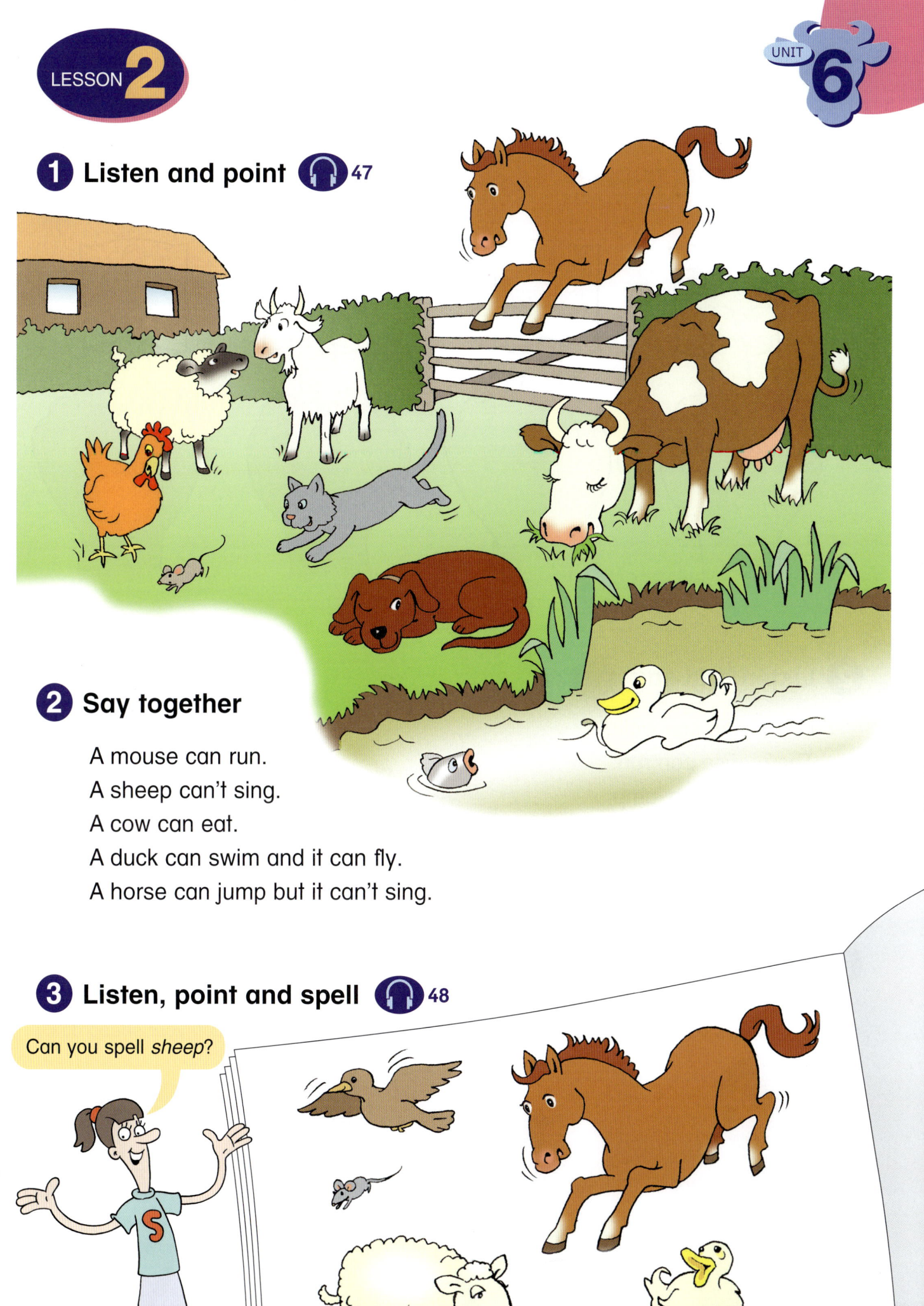

47

1 Make finger puppets → Activity Book cut-out 6

2 Listen and say  49

The sheep can walk.
The mouse can run.
The horse can jump.
The duck can swim.
The chicken can't fly.

Can you make this?

3 Do it together

Look, my duck is swimming.
What's your duck doing?

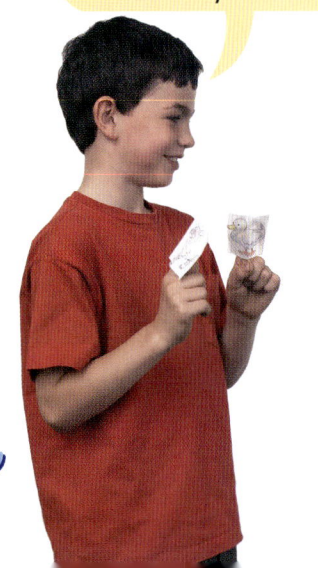

What can your sheep do?

UNIT 6 — LESSON 5

1 Listen and look 🎧 52

- Can you see the bird?
- Yes, it's on the goat.

2 Listen, choose and answer together 🎧 53

sheep   cow   frog   mouse   duck

Point to the chicken.

3 Read and point

Point to the bird on the goat.
Point to the goat next to the cow.
Point to the cat in the tree.
Point to the spider under the horse.
Point to the dog under the tree.

LESSON 6

1 Look again

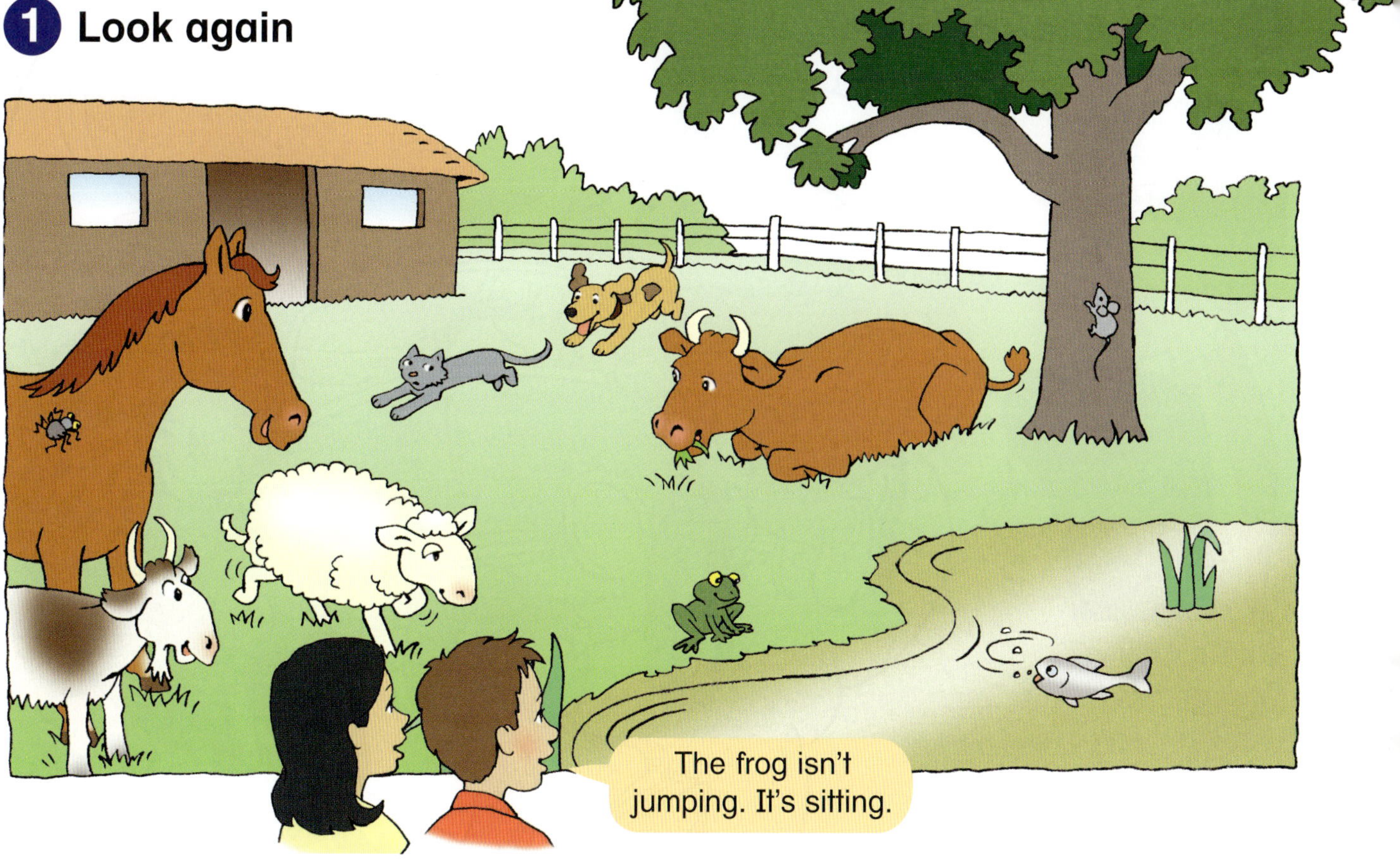

The frog isn't jumping. It's sitting.

2 Match the questions and answers

1 Is the fish in the pond?
2 Where's the spider?
3 Is the cat in the tree?
4 What's the dog doing?
5 Is the goat running?

a No, it isn't.
b Yes, it is.
c It's running.
d No, it's standing next to the horse.
e It's on the horse.

3 Let's play *What am I?*

UNIT 6

LESSON 7

1 Point and say

What's this?

It's a hippo.

What's it doing?

It's riding a bike!

2 Ask and answer

1 Is the tiger flying a plane?
2 Is the spider riding a motorbike?
3 Is the elephant driving a car?
4 Is the hippo riding a bike?
5 Is the snake watching TV?

3 Answer for you

1 Can you fly?
2 Can you jump?
3 Can you swim?
4 Can you run?
5 Have you got a dog?
6 Have you got a cat?

1 Listen and say 🎧 54

| my fly | walk talk | eat feet | run fun |

2 Listen and sing 🎧 55

Birds can fly,
Up in the sky.
Frogs can jump,
Very, very high.

Ducks can swim,
Birds can sing,
Dogs can walk,
And I can talk.

Animals can run,
And I can have fun.
Animals can eat
And I can jump with my feet.

3 Play *Draw the farm*

Draw a bird in the tree.

UNIT 7 The classroom

LESSON 1

1 Listen and repeat  56

2 Read and say *yes* or *no*

1 Is Sam's desk in front of the table?
2 Is the teacher writing questions in a book?
3 Is Kim writing the answers?
4 Has Sam got his pencil?
5 Is Sam's pencil in his bag?

3 Say and spell

school

classroom

question

sentence

54

1 Listen and point  57

2 Say together

Miss Green's standing in front of the class.
Sam's pen's on the floor.
Sam's behind the table.
The books are on the desk.
The desk's next to the door.

3 Listen, point and spell 58

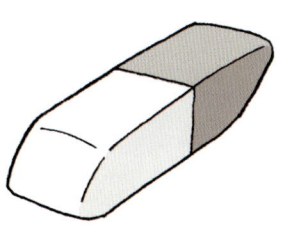

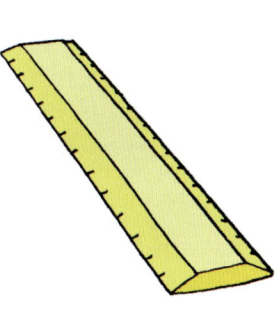

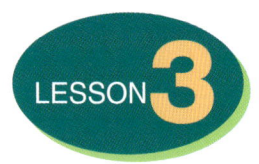

1 Make a classroom picture → Activity Book cut-out 7

Can you make this?

2 Listen and say 🎧 59

The book's on the desk.
The pen's in the bag.
The pencil's behind the eraser.
The ruler's under the chair.
The picture's next to the board.

3 Do it together

Draw a bag next to the table.

Draw a book under the desk.

UNIT 7

1 Listen, look and remember 🎧 60

Where's the yellow book?

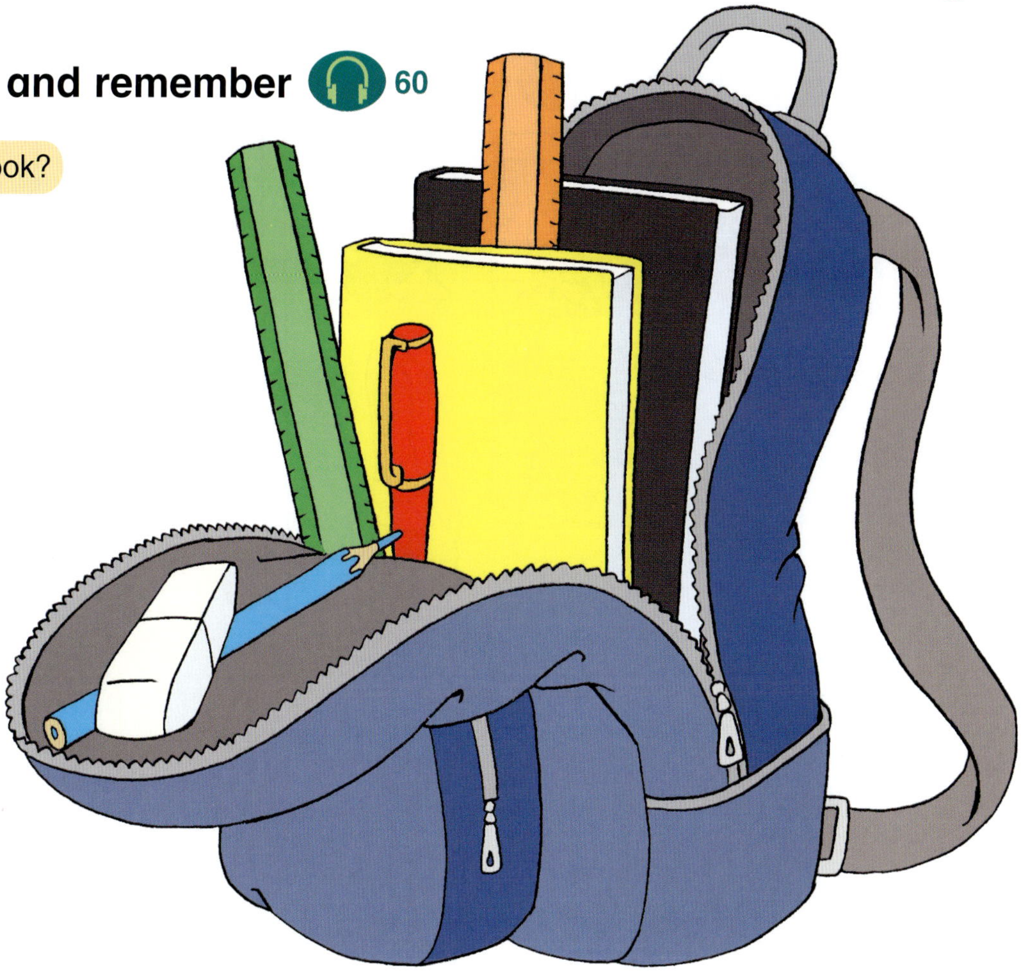

2 Listen and say *yes* or *no* 🎧 61

3 Play a game

Is the book next to the pen?

No. Is the eraser under the ruler?

What's in your school bag?

UNIT 7   LESSON 5

There are eight books on the table.

1 Listen and look 🎧 62

2 Listen, choose and answer together 63

the zoo

looking at the picture

on the wall

the snakes

eight

Is it big or small?

3 Read and point

Point to the crocodiles.
Point to the snakes.
Point to the pens on the desk.
Point to the books on the table.
Point to the rulers on the floor.

58

LESSON 6

UNIT **7**

"The crocodiles are between the tiger and the snakes."

1 Look again

2 Match the questions and answers

1 What colour are the crocodiles?   a They're on the floor.
2 How many snakes can you see?   b Three rulers.
3 What's on the chair?   c Four.
4 Where are the books?   d They're blue.
5 What's the tiger doing?   e It's sitting down.

3 Let's play
Find the pen

"Where's the pen?"
"Is it behind the bookcase?"

UNIT 7

LESSON 7

1 Point and say

Number nineteen is a word.

Number eighteen is a tick.

Number twenty is a sentence.

2 Ask and answer

1 What's number nine?
2 What's number fourteen?
3 What's number sixteen?
4 Which number is the letter *b*?
5 Which number is the cross?
6 Which number is the word *class*?

3 Answer for you

1 Where's your teacher?
2 Who's sitting next to you?
3 Are you next to the door?
4 Who's sitting in front of the window?
5 Where are your books?
6 What's in your school bag?

lesson 8

1 Listen and say 🎧 64

- look   book
- your   door

2 Listen and sing 🎧 65 ♪♫♪♫

Let's go to school and read our books,
Read our books, read our books.
Let's go to school and read our books,
In our new classroom.

Let's go to school and write our names,
Write our names, write our names.
Let's go to school and write our names,
In our Super Starters books.

3 Play *Where's the bag?*

Where's the bag?

Here it is, next to the board.

bag
cross (✘)
tick (✔)
book
board
desk
pencil
ruler
teacher
table

61

UNIT 8 Sport and hobbies

1 Listen and repeat 🎧 66

2 Read and say *yes* or *no*

1 Sam's got a bike.
2 Kim can't ride a bike.
3 Sam likes swimming.
4 Swimming is Ann's favourite sport.
5 They can go swimming.

3 Say and spell

baseball   hockey   badminton   basketball

LESSON 2

UNIT 8

1 Listen and point 🎧 67

2 Say together

There's one boy playing basketball.
There's one man swimming.
There are two girls playing tennis.
There are two men riding bikes.
There are four boys playing football and six girls playing hockey.

3 Listen, point and spell 🎧 68

These words have double letters.

1 **Make a sports spinner** → Activity Book cut-out 8

Can you make this?

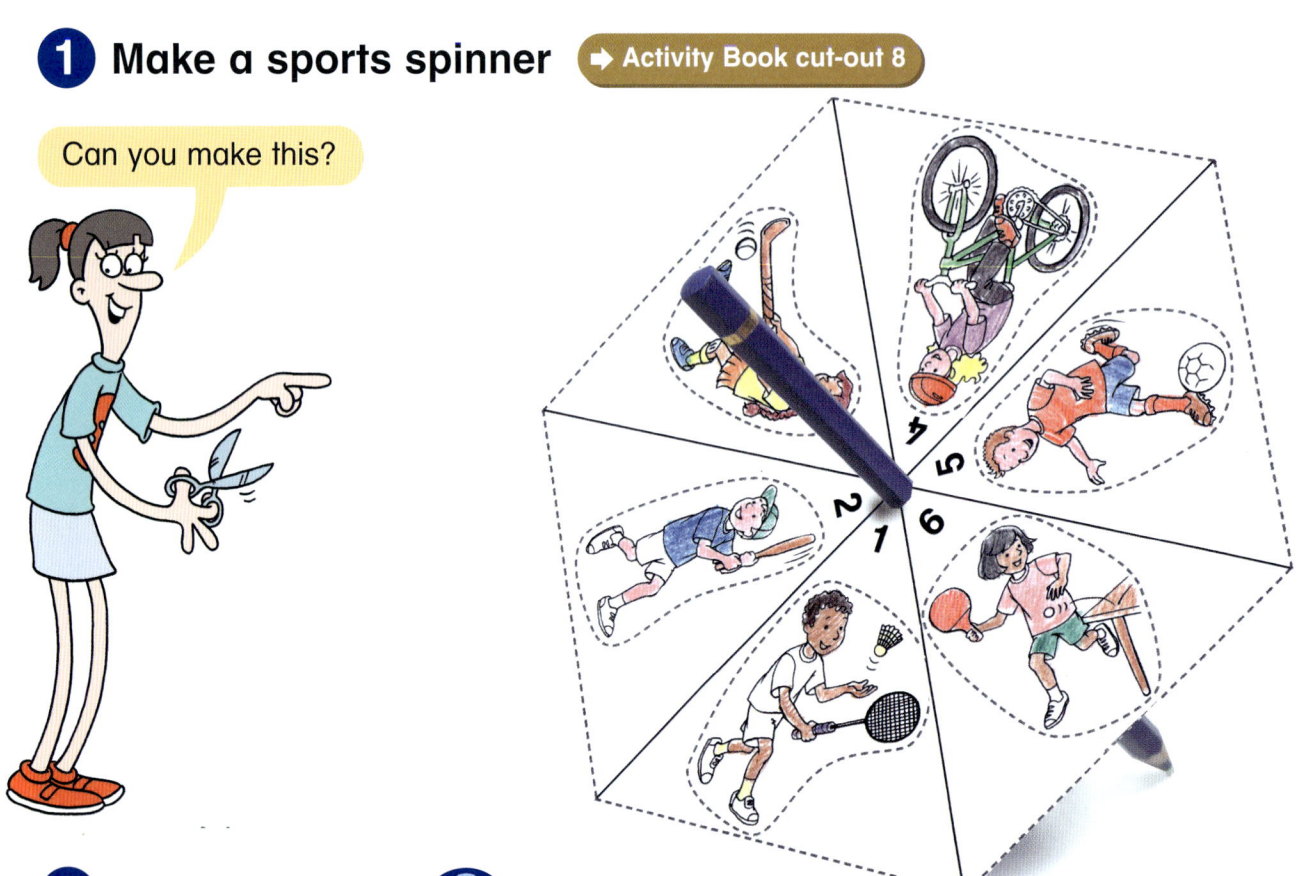

2 **Listen and say** 🎧 69

Number 1's playing badminton. He's wearing a white T-shirt and white shorts.
Number 4's riding a bike. She's wearing black trousers and a purple T-shirt.
Number 6's playing table tennis. She's wearing green shorts and a pink T-shirt.

3 **Do it together**

What's he doing?

He's playing football.

UNIT 8

LESSON 5

1 Listen and look  72

What's Joe doing?

He's kicking a football.

2 Listen, choose and answer together  73

bouncing a ball   running   kicking a football   jumping

3 Read and point

Point to the boy kicking a ball.
Point to the girl catching a ball.
Point to the boy throwing a ball.
Point to the girl jumping.

I'm jumping.

LESSON 6 · UNIT 8

1 Look again

Sue's bouncing a ball.

2 Match the questions and answers

1 What's Bill doing?   a She's throwing a ball.
2 What's Liz doing?   b Sue's bouncing a ball.
3 Who's kicking a ball?   c Nick's jumping.
4 Who's bouncing a ball?   d Ann's kicking a ball.
5 Is Nick jumping or running? e He's catching a ball.

3 Let's play *Go!*

She's catching a ball.

UNIT 8 — LESSON 7

1 Point and say

He's wearing a yellow shirt.
He's playing baseball.

She's wearing a white skirt.
She's playing tennis.

2 Ask and answer

1 What's the boy wearing a red T-shirt playing?
2 Which girl is playing badminton?
3 What's the man wearing green doing?
4 What's the girl wearing a black hat doing? .
5 Which man is playing table tennis?
6 What's the girl wearing blue shorts doing?

I like playing baseball.

3 Answer for you

1 Do you like playing badminton?
2 Do you like swimming?
3 Do you like playing basketball?
4 Can you play the guitar?
5 What's your favourite sport?
6 What's your favourite hobby?

1 Listen and say 🎧 74

| football   basketball   baseball | swimming   riding   fishing |

2 Listen and sing 🎧 75

I play hockey. I play tennis.
I play football and have a lovely time!

You go swimming. You go riding.
You go running and have a lovely time!

We like fishing. We like baseball.
We like singing and having a lovely time!

Running, jumping, kicking a ball,
I like playing with you all!

3 Play *Who are you?*

Do you like swimming?

Yes.

Do you like playing tennis?

No.

Do you like playing basketball?

Yes.

Are you Kim?

Yes.

	Kim	Sam	Bob	Ann
hockey	✔	✔	✘	✔
basketball	✔	✘	✔	✘
tennis	✘	✔	✔	✘
badminton	✘	✘	✘	✔
ride a horse	✔	✘	✘	✔
swimming	✔	✔	✘	✔
football	✘	✔	✔	✘
fishing	✘	✘	✔	✘

69

UNIT 9 Food and drink

LESSON 1

1 Listen and repeat 🎧 76

2 Read and say *yes* or *no*

1. Kim likes burgers and fries.
2. Kim likes chicken.
3. Sam loves chicken.
4. Sam wants a big mango ice cream.
5. Kim wants a big lemon ice cream.
6. Sam has got a lot of food.

3 Say and spell

burger

fries

mango

lemon

70

1 Listen and point 🎧 77

2 Say together

I like chicken with rice and carrots.
Kim likes burgers, fries and onions.
Sam likes chicken and rice.
They like lemon and lime ice cream.

3 Listen, point and spell 🎧 78

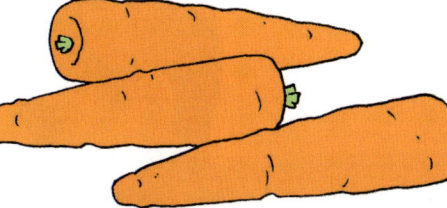

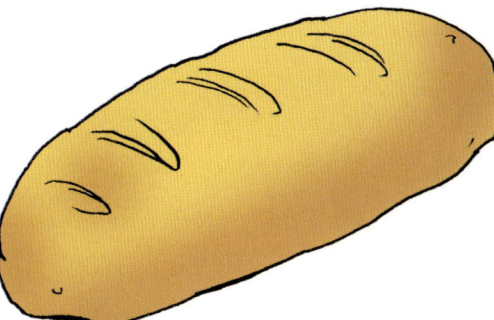

UNIT 9

LESSON 3

1 Make a lunch plate → Activity Book cut-out 9

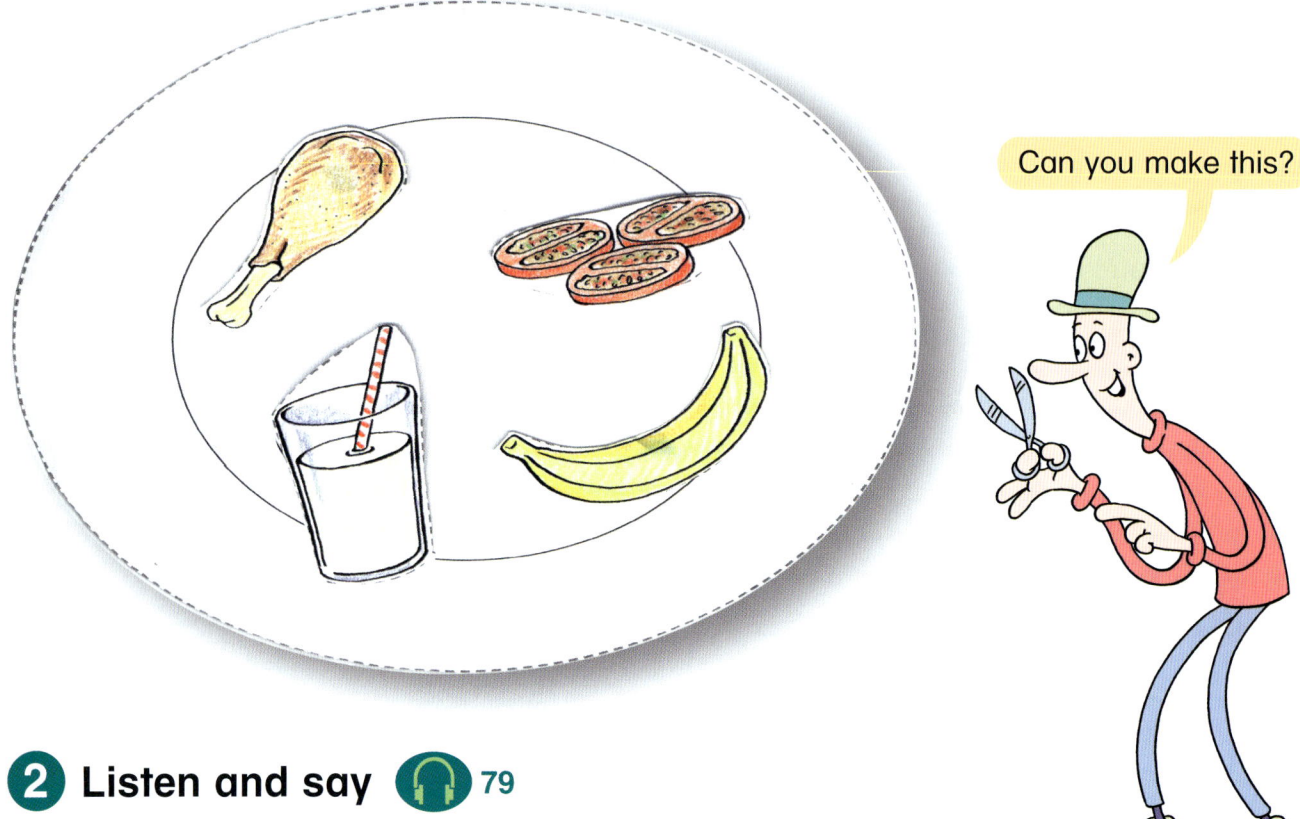

Can you make this?

2 Listen and say 🎧 79

What are you having for lunch?
I'm having chicken, peas, rice and milk.
And what are you having for lunch?
I'm having a burger, a banana and some orange juice.

3 Do it together

Are you having chicken?

No, I'm not. Are you having rice?

Yes, I am.

72

LESSON 4

UNIT 9

1 Listen, look and remember 🎧 80

2 Listen and say *yes* or *no* 🎧 81

What are they eating?

3 Play a game

UNIT 9

LESSON 5

1 Listen and look  82

I'm eating a burger.

I'm eating an apple.

2 Listen, choose and answer together  83

Yes, that's right.

No, that isn't right.

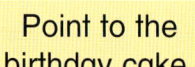
Point to the birthday cake.

3 Read and point

Point to the girl throwing a balloon.
Point to the boy catching a balloon.
Point to the man drinking lemonade.
Point to the girl eating an apple.
Point to the birthday cake.

1 Look again

Kim isn't eating an apple. She's eating an egg.

2 Match the questions and answers

1 What's Ann doing?
2 What's Dad eating?
3 What's Mum drinking?
4 What are Ben and Tom doing?
5 Who's eating birthday cake?
6 How many candles are on the birthday cake?

a There are eight candles.
b They're playing football.
c He's eating chicken.
d She's drinking water.
e She's playing table tennis.
f Grandma is.

3 Let's play *What's for supper?*

Are we having chicken for supper?

Yes.

My supper menu
chicken and fries
grapes
watermelon
cake
pear juice

UNIT 9 — LESSON 7

1 Point and say

For breakfast, I eat eggs and bread.

For lunch, I eat chicken, rice and carrots.

For dinner, I eat fish, potatoes and peas.

2 Ask and answer

1. What does Kim eat for breakfast?
2. What does Dad drink for lunch?
3. What does Mum eat for dinner?
4. Who eats chicken for lunch?
5. Who drinks milk for breakfast?

I love cake!

3 Answer for you

1. What do you eat for lunch?
2. What do you eat for breakfast?
3. What do you like eating for dinner?
4. What's your favourite fruit?
5. What's your favourite drink?

LESSON 8

UNIT 9

1 Listen and say  84

- ice cream   beans
- rice   nice
- cake   make
- meat   feet
- pears   wears

2 Listen and sing 85

1 I like beans for my breakfast.
   I like beans!
   I like eggs for my breakfast.
   I like beans and eggs.

2 He likes cake for his lunch.
   He likes cake!
   He likes ice cream for his lunch.
   He likes cake and ice cream.

3 She likes meat for her dinner.
   She likes meat.
   She likes rice for her dinner.
   She likes meat and rice.

4 They like pears for their supper.
   They like pears.
   They like grapes for their supper.
   They like pears and grapes.

5 And we like ...

3 Play *Who's got it?*

Who's got the carrots?

UNIT 10 In the house

LESSON 1

1 Listen and repeat 🎧 86

I live in a small flat.

2 Read and say *yes* or *no*

1 Sam's got a new house.
2 Kim lives in a flat.
3 Sam lives at number 11, Blue Street.
4 Sam's house is next to Kim's house.
5 Sam's house hasn't got many windows.
6 Sam's house has got a funny front door.

3 Say and spell

| house | flat | room | number |

LESSON 2

UNIT 10

1 Listen and point 🎧 87

2 Say together

There's a kitchen and a bathroom.
There are three bedrooms.
The dining room's next to the living room.
There's a hall between the living room and the kitchen.
There's a big garden.

3 Listen, point and spell 🎧 88

How do you spell 'hall'?

79

1 **Make a bedroom**

Can you make this?

2 **Listen and say**  89

The doll's on the bed.
The mat's in front of the cupboard.
The lamp's on the table.
The radio's in the cupboard.
The mirror's next to the cupboard.

3 **Do it together**

Where's your doll?

It's in the box.

What colour's your bed?

It's purple.

Where's your radio?

It's under the chair.

LESSON 4

UNIT 10

1 Listen, look and remember 🎧 90

2 Listen and say *yes* or *no* 🎧 91

3 Play a game

Find the toy.

Is it on the bed?

No.

Is it under the table?

Yes.

UNIT **10**

LESSON **5**

1 Listen and look 🎧 92

"This is my new house."

2 Listen, choose and answer together 🎧 93

Sam blue in the living room a horse
in the bathroom

3 Read and point

Point to the blue armchair.
Point to the big bath.
Point to the piano.
Point to the photo of the baby.
Point to the toy horse.

"Is she happy or sad?"

LESSON 6

UNIT 10

1 Look again

There's a robot in the box.

2 Match the questions and answers

1 Is the armchair red or blue?
2 What's in the painting?
3 Is the sofa in the living room or in the dining room?
4 Where's the cat?
5 Is the bath big or small?
6 What's in the box?

a A beach.
b It's small.
c It's red.
d It's in the dining room.
e A robot.
f It's under the table.

3 Let's play *Where's the clock?*

Put the clock on the bookcase.

UNIT 10

LESSON 7

1 Listen, point and say 🎧 94

1 a   b

2 a   b

3 a   b

4 a   b

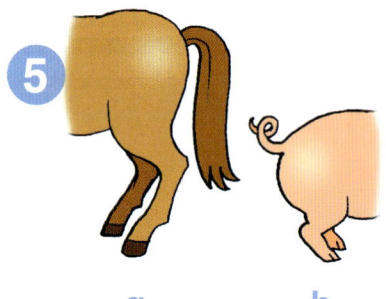
5 a   b

6 a   b

7 a   b

2 Ask and answer

1 Which house is big?
2 What colour's the dirty sofa?
3 Is the horse's tail long or short?
4 What's the beautiful doll wearing?
5 What colour's the small house?
6 Who's sad?

3 Answer for you

1 Do you live in a house?
2 How many bedrooms are there?
3 Have you got a TV in your bedroom?
4 Have you got a sofa in your house?
5 What colour is it?
6 Have you got a garden?

Is your house new or old?

LESSON 8

UNIT 10

1 Listen and say 🎧 95

look book		two too		see me

house mouse		door floor		he tree

2 Listen and sing 🎧 96 ♪ ♪ ♪ ♪

1 Here's my house,
   With a door and a window, too.
   Come and see our very big tree,
   And play a game or two.

2 Here's my bedroom,
   With a bed and a bookcase, too.
   Come and see and play with me,
   And read a book or two.

3 Here's our kitchen,
   With chairs and a table, too.
   Come and see and stay for tea,
   And have some dinner, too!

3 Play *Snap*

Sofa.

Snap!

85